WEALTH TOPICAL BIBLE

Christian T. Howell Sr.

Copyright © 2019 Christian Howell Sr.

All scriptures are taken from King James Version unless otherwise indicated.

Scriptures are taken from the KING JAMES VERSION (KJV):
KING JAMES VERSION, public domain.

Scripture quotations taken from the Amplified® Bible (AMP),
Copyright © 2015 by The Lockman Foundation
Used by permission. www.Lockman.org

All rights reserved. This book or any portion thereof may not be reproduced or used in any manner whatsoever without the express written permission of the publisher except for the use of brief quotations in a book review.

ISBN: 978-1-7337342-2-6 (Paperback)

First printing, 2019

Christian Howell Sr.
P.O. Box 2995
Riverview, FL 33569

www.overcomersmovement.org

Introduction

Wealth, in most cultures, is often viewed as a sign of affluence or status. It has been pursued by many, across every generation, in an attempt to resolve issues of esteem, personal value, private ambitions, desires, and goals. And with all of the striving for wealth in the earth, conflicts and wars have resulted, and alliances have been forged that continually shape the landscape and cultures around the globe. Despite all of the quests to obtain and pass on wealth, a lot of it has been done with little to no understanding of true wealth nor its principles.

Oftentimes, wealth is defined in our culture as a large amount of money or possessions, or an abundance of valuable resources or material possessions. To make this definition even more simple, our modern understanding of wealth is tied to money and earthly treasures. This simple and primitive understanding leads to false practices and beliefs, and usually fuels passion and desire to obtain money with little purpose – and totally violating the principles of wealth.

If wealth is associated with money or currency, then the Bible clearly states that all of the gold and silver belong to God (Haggai 2:8). This clearly defines Him as the wealthiest King to ever live! Also, as the Owner of all of the currency, He alone controls the principles and policies that determine how it works and how it flows. So, to pursue and work to earn or control wealth, without using His methods and principles seem all but useless to me.

Money is the currency or the thing used as an exchange or payment for services or items. While it is advantageous to possess it, it has a different value in each country or society. Even more, the value of money is not the same in every culture or generation. In America, the value of the dollar is not the same as it is in Europe or Africa. Furthermore, what it's worth today is not the same as it was during the Great Depression. Simply stated, the value of money fluctuates. Hopefully, you see and agree that there must be something more significant than money – it is wealth.

The Bible uses different words when referring to wealth. Some include money, wealth, riches, might, goods, and treasure. While other words are used interchangeably, the primary meaning of the word is derived from the Hebrew language "chayil". This word gives greater clarity and understanding of the topic at hand. The meaning of "chayil" expands it from merely an external tool used to make a transaction to a force, resource, or influence on the inside that generates resources on the outside (externally). In light of the other words that the scriptures use for wealth, we can understand that the Bible is full of principles, wisdom, and strategies concerning wealth.

Wealth is a power or force given to believers (covenant-keepers) as a sign of the covenant and relationship between the King and His subjects…the Father and His children (Deut 8:18). It is a distinguishing and recognizable factor that marks us and makes us attractive to other people. You could consider it a recruiting tool that gets the attention of other people who are not properly aligned with our King. Because it is granted and bestowed by the King, true wealth gives no room for arrogance, pride, or laziness. Wealth requires an understanding of purpose and stewardship.

All of the resources that are assigned to you are designed to be used according to who you are and what you were created to do. Every day that you are alive, God gives you more than enough time, ideas, money, and strength to be successful in that day. It just has to properly managed and allocated so that you never run out and more importantly, live with an abundance of resources that amount to stored up wealth (John 10:10).

The greatest form of wealth that you may ever receive usually come in the form of a "seed". Seeds are the beginning part of life. Humans, begin in seed form. Plants and trees begin in seed form. Fruits begin in seed form. Even animals begin in some form of a seed. Read this very carefully… God often releases wealth in the seed form called dreams, ideas, witty inventions, and solutions to problems in society. Money is usually the reward, but wealth is generated when we properly steward the ideas, concepts, strategies, and businesses that God gives to us in seed form.

The real secret strategy of obtaining and maintaining wealth is not in how much you gather, nor in how much you save, it is in how much you sow. AND in the soil that you place your seed in. Everything in the Kingdom works off of the principle of sowing and reaping. Galatians 6:7 says "Do not be deceived, God is not mocked [He will not allow Himself to be ridiculed, nor treated with contempt nor allow His precepts to be scornfully set aside]; for whatever a man sows, this and this only is what he will reap" (Amp).

My friend, with this understanding, you are only one idea or thought away from becoming wealthy. My prayer for you is that the God-given thoughts and ideas on the inside of you become money and currency on the outside of you. I pray that you receive a fresh download and impartation from the Creator that will radically revolutionalize your life. Finally, I pray that you break all cycles of poverty, hopelessness, and despair with the seeds that you sow – and that they create a legacy of wealth that endures from generation to generation.

CONFESSIONS OF WEALTH

I have the Mind of Christ; therefore, I have wealthy thoughts that produce wealth and riches in my life.

Wealth and riches are in my hands, my family's hands…and for generations to come.

I break covenant and generational curses that are tied to poverty and destruction off my life and my family's lives, including the next three generations to come.

I have a wealthy and productive mind; therefore, I am free of distraction and disorganization that would drain my life and my resources.

My soul is healed and made whole; therefore I prosper in every area of my life.

Wealth and riches are in my house. My pantry and cupboards will never see lack.

Like Naomi, people of great influence and wealth are looking for me now.

I have wisdom and understanding that is from above. It preserves and protects my wealth that is granted from God.

My God-given wealth is a defense and shield for me.

I possess an abundance of peace, love, joy, and righteousness in the Holy Ghost.

I have an abundance of seeds. I sow freely from my wealth.

God, I thank You that according to Your riches in heaven, You generously provide everything I need. In fact, I have more than enough so that I can share my extra with the those in need.

WEALTH

OLD TESTAMENT

Genesis 34:29 And all their wealth, and all their little ones, and their wives took they captive, and spoiled even all that was in the house.

Deuteronomy 8:17 And thou say in thine heart, My power and the might of mine hand hath gotten me this wealth.

Deuteronomy 8:18 But thou shalt remember the LORD thy God: for it is he that giveth thee power to get wealth, that he may establish his covenant which he sware unto thy fathers, as it is this day.

Ruth 2:1 And Naomi had a kinsman of her husband's, a mighty man of wealth, of the family of Elimelech; and his name was Boaz.

1 Samuel 2:32 And thou shalt see an enemy in my habitation, in all the wealth which God shall give Israel: and there shall not be an old man in thine house for ever.

2 Kings 15:20 And Menahem exacted the money of Israel, even of all the mighty men of wealth, of each man fifty shekels of silver, to give to the king of Assyria. So the king of Assyria turned back, and stayed not there in the land.

2 Chronicles 1:11 And God said to Solomon, Because this was in thine heart, and thou hast not asked riches, wealth, or honour, nor the life of thine enemies, neither yet hast asked long life; but hast asked wisdom and knowledge for thyself, that thou mayest judge my people, over whom I have made thee king:

2 Chronicles 1:12 Wisdom and knowledge is granted unto thee; and I will give thee riches, and wealth, and honour, such as none

of the kings have had that have been before thee, neither shall there any after thee have the like.

Ezra 9:12 Now therefore give not your daughters unto their sons, neither take their daughters unto your sons, nor seek their peace or their wealth for ever: that ye may be strong, and eat the good of the land, and leave it for an inheritance to your children for ever.

Esther 10:3 For Mordecai the Jew was next unto king Ahasuerus, and great among the Jews, and accepted of the multitude of his brethren, seeking the wealth of his people, and speaking peace to all his seed.

Job 21:13 They spend their days in wealth, and in a moment go down to the grave.

Job 31:25 If I rejoiced because my wealth was great, and because mine hand had gotten much;

Psalms 44:12 Thou sellest thy people for nought, and dost not increase thy wealth by their price.

Psalms 49:6 They that trust in their wealth, and boast themselves in the multitude of their riches;

Psalms 49:10 For he seeth that wise men die, likewise the fool and the brutish person perish, and leave their wealth to others.

Psalms 112:3 Wealth and riches shall be in his house: and his righteousness endureth for ever.

Proverbs 5:10 Lest strangers be filled with thy wealth; and thy labours be in the house of a stranger;

Proverbs 10:15 The rich man's wealth is his strong city: the destruction of the poor is their poverty.

Proverbs 13:11 Wealth gotten by vanity shall be diminished: but he that gathereth by labour shall increase.

Proverbs 13:22 A good man leaveth an inheritance to his children's children: and the wealth of the sinner is laid up for the just.

Proverbs 18:11 The rich man's wealth is his strong city, and as an high wall in his own conceit.

Proverbs 19:4 Wealth maketh many friends; but the poor is separated from his neighbour.

Ecclesiastes 5:19 Every man also to whom God hath given riches and wealth, and hath given him power to eat thereof, and to take his portion, and to rejoice in his labour; this is the gift of God.

Ecclesiastes 6:2 A man to whom God hath given riches, wealth, and honour, so that he wanteth nothing for his soul of all that he desireth, yet God giveth him not power to eat thereof, but a stranger eateth it: this is vanity, and it is an evil disease.

Zechariah 14:14 And Judah also shall fight at Jerusalem; and the wealth of all the heathen round about shall be gathered together, gold, and silver, and apparel, in great abundance.

NEW TESTAMENT

Acts 19:25 Whom he called together with the workmen of like occupation, and said, Sirs, ye know that by this craft we have our wealth.

1 Corinthians 10:24 Let no man seek his own, but every man another's wealth.

ABUNDANCE

OLD TESTAMENT

Deuteronomy 28:47 Because thou servedst not the LORD thy God with joyfulness, and with gladness of heart, for the abundance of all things;

Deuteronomy 33:19 They shall call the people unto the mountain; there they shall offer sacrifices of righteousness: for they shall suck of the abundance of the seas, and of treasures hid in the sand.

1 Samuel 1:16 Count not thine handmaid for a daughter of Belial: for out of the abundance of my complaint and grief have I spoken hitherto.

2 Samuel 12:30 And he took their king's crown from off his head, the weight whereof was a talent of gold with the precious stones: and it was set on David's head. And he brought forth the spoil of the city in great abundance.

1 Kings 1:19 And he hath slain oxen and fat cattle and sheep in abundance, and hath called all the sons of the king, and Abiathar the priest, and Joab the captain of the host: but Solomon thy servant hath he not called.

1 Kings 1:25 For he is gone down this day, and hath slain oxen and fat cattle and sheep in abundance, and hath called all the king's sons, and the captains of the host, and Abiathar the priest; and, behold, they eat and drink before him, and say, God save king Adonijah.

1 Kings 10:10 And she gave the king an hundred and twenty talents of gold, and of spices very great store, and precious stones: there came no more such abundance of spices as these which the queen of Sheba gave to king Solomon.

1 Kings 10:27 And the king made silver to be in Jerusalem as stones, and cedars made he to be as the sycomore trees that are in the vale, for abundance.

1 Kings 18:41 And Elijah said unto Ahab, Get thee up, eat and drink; for there is a sound of abundance of rain.

1 Chronicles 22:3 And David prepared iron in abundance for the nails for the doors of the gates, and for the joinings; and brass in abundance without weight;

1 Chronicles 22:4 Also cedar trees in abundance: for the Zidonians and they of Tyre brought much cedar wood to David.

1 Chronicles 22:14 Now, behold, in my trouble I have prepared for the house of the LORD an hundred thousand talents of gold, and a thousand thousand talents of silver; and of brass and iron without weight; for it is in abundance: timber also and stone have I prepared; and thou mayest add thereto.

1 Chronicles 22:15 Moreover there are workmen with thee in abundance, hewers and workers of stone and timber, and all manner of cunning men for every manner of work.

1 Chronicles 29:2 Now I have prepared with all my might for the house of my God the gold for things to be made of gold, and the silver for things of silver, and the brass for things of brass, the iron for things of iron, and wood for things of wood; onyx stones, and stones to be set, glistering stones, and of divers colours, and all manner of precious stones, and marble stones in abundance.

1 Chronicles 29:21 And they sacrificed sacrifices unto the LORD, and offered burnt offerings unto the LORD, on the morrow after that day, even a thousand bullocks, a thousand

rams, and a thousand lambs, with their drink offerings, and sacrifices in abundance for all Israel:

2 Chronicles 1:15 And the king made silver and gold at Jerusalem as plenteous as stones, and cedar trees made he as the sycomore trees that are in the vale for abundance.

2 Chronicles 2:9 Even to prepare me timber in abundance: for the house which I am about to build shall be wonderful great.

2 Chronicles 4:18 Thus Solomon made all these vessels in great abundance: for the weight of the brass could not be found out.

2 Chronicles 9:1 And when the queen of Sheba heard of the fame of Solomon, she came to prove Solomon with hard questions at Jerusalem, with a very great company, and camels that bare spices, and gold in abundance, and precious stones: and when she was come to Solomon, she communed with him of all that was in her heart.

2 Chronicles 9:9 And she gave the king an hundred and twenty talents of gold, and of spices great abundance, and precious stones: neither was there any such spice as the queen of Sheba gave king Solomon.

2 Chronicles 9:27 And the king made silver in Jerusalem as stones, and cedar trees made he as the sycomore trees that are in the low plains in abundance.

2 Chronicles 11:23 And he dealt wisely, and dispersed of all his children throughout all the countries of Judah and Benjamin, unto every fenced city: and he gave them victual in abundance. And he desired many wives.

2 Chronicles 14:15 They smote also the tents of cattle, and carried away sheep and camels in abundance, and returned to Jerusalem.

2 Chronicles 15:9 And he gathered all Judah and Benjamin, and the strangers with them out of Ephraim and Manasseh, and out of Simeon: for they fell to him out of Israel in abundance, when they saw that the LORD his God was with him.

2 Chronicles 17:5 Therefore the LORD stablished the kingdom in his hand; and all Judah brought to Jehoshaphat presents; and he had riches and honour in abundance.

2 Chronicles 18:1 Now Jehoshaphat had riches and honour in abundance, and joined affinity with Ahab.

2 Chronicles 18:2 And after certain years he went down to Ahab to Samaria. And Ahab killed sheep and oxen for him in abundance, and for the people that he had with him, and persuaded him to go up with him to Ramothgilead.

2 Chronicles 20:25 And when Jehoshaphat and his people came to take away the spoil of them, they found among them in abundance both riches with the dead bodies, and precious jewels, which they stripped off for themselves, more than they could carry away: and they were three days in gathering of the spoil, it was so much.

2 Chronicles 24:11 Now it came to pass, that at what time the chest was brought unto the king's office by the hand of the Levites, and when they saw that there was much money, the king's scribe and the high priest's officer came and emptied the chest, and took it, and carried it to his place again. Thus they did day by day, and gathered money in abundance.

2 Chronicles 29:35 And also the burnt offerings were in abundance, with the fat of the peace offerings, and the drink offerings for every burnt offering. So the service of the house of the LORD was set in order.

2 Chronicles 31:5 And as soon as the commandment came abroad, the children of Israel brought in abundance the firstfruits of corn, wine, and oil, and honey, and of all the increase of the field; and the tithe of all things brought they in abundantly.

2 Chronicles 32:5 Also he strengthened himself, and built up all the wall that was broken, and raised it up to the towers, and another wall without, and repaired Millo in the city of David, and made darts and shields in abundance.

2 Chronicles 32:29 Moreover he provided him cities, and possessions of flocks and herds in abundance: for God had given him substance very much.

Nehemiah 9:25 And they took strong cities, and a fat land, and possessed houses full of all goods, wells digged, vineyards, and oliveyards, and fruit trees in abundance: so they did eat, and were filled, and became fat, and delighted themselves in thy great goodness.

Esther 1:7 And they gave them drink in vessels of gold, (the vessels being diverse one from another,) and royal wine in abundance, according to the state of the king.

Job 22:11 Or darkness, that thou canst not see; and abundance of waters cover thee.

Job 36:31 For by them judgeth he the people; he giveth meat in abundance.

Job 38:34 Canst thou lift up thy voice to the clouds, that abundance of waters may cover thee?

Psalms 37:11 But the meek shall inherit the earth; and shall delight themselves in the abundance of peace.

Psalms 52:7 Lo, this is the man that made not God his strength; but trusted in the abundance of his riches, and strengthened himself in his wickedness.

Psalms 72:7 In his days shall the righteous flourish; and abundance of peace so long as the moon endureth.

Psalms 105:30 Their land brought forth frogs in abundance, in the chambers of their kings.

Ecclesiastes 5:10 He that loveth silver shall not be satisfied with silver; nor he that loveth abundance with increase: this is also vanity.

Ecclesiastes 5:12 The sleep of a labouring man is sweet, whether he eat little or much: but the abundance of the rich will not suffer him to sleep.

Isaiah 7:22 And it shall come to pass, for the abundance of milk that they shall give he shall eat butter: for butter and honey shall every one eat that is left in the land.

Isaiah 15:7 Therefore the abundance they have gotten, and that which they have laid up, shall they carry away to the brook of the willows.

Isaiah 47:9 But these two things shall come to thee in a moment in one day, the loss of children, and widowhood: they shall come upon thee in their perfection for the multitude of thy sorceries, and for the great abundance of thine enchantments.

Isaiah 60:5 Then thou shalt see, and flow together, and thine heart shall fear, and be enlarged; because the abundance of the sea shall be converted unto thee, the forces of the Gentiles shall come unto thee.

Isaiah 66:11 That ye may suck, and be satisfied with the breasts of her consolations; that ye may milk out, and be delighted with the abundance of her glory.

Jeremiah 33:6 Behold, I will bring it health and cure, and I will cure them, and will reveal unto them the abundance of peace and truth.

Ezekiel 16:49 Behold, this was the iniquity of thy sister Sodom, pride, fulness of bread, and abundance of idleness was in her and in her daughters, neither did she strengthen the hand of the poor and needy.

Ezekiel 26:10 By reason of the abundance of his horses their dust shall cover thee: thy walls shall shake at the noise of the horsemen, and of the wheels, and of the chariots, when he shall enter into thy gates, as men enter into a city wherein is made a breach.

Zecheriah 14:14 And Judah also shall fight at Jerusalem; and the wealth of all the heathen round about shall be gathered together, gold, and silver, and apparel, in great abundance.

NEW TESTAMENT

Matthew 12:34 O generation of vipers, how can ye, being evil, speak good things? for out of the abundance of the heart the mouth speaketh.

Matthew 13:12 For whosoever hath, to him shall be given, and he shall have more abundance: but whosoever hath not, from him shall be taken away even that he hath.

Matthew 25:29 For unto every one that hath shall be given, and he shall have abundance: but from him that hath not shall be taken away even that which he hath.

Mark 12:44 For all they did cast in of their abundance; but she of her want did cast in all that she had, even all her living.

Luke 6:45 A good man out of the good treasure of his heart bringeth forth that which is good; and an evil man out of the evil treasure of his heart bringeth forth that which is evil: for of the abundance of the heart his mouth speaketh.

Luke 12:15 And he said unto them, Take heed, and beware of covetousness: for a man's life consisteth not in the abundance of the things which he possesseth.

Luke 21:4 For all these have of their abundance cast in unto the offerings of God: but she of her penury hath cast in all the living that she had.

Romans 5:17 For if by one man's offence death reigned by one; much more they which receive abundance of grace and of the gift of righteousness shall reign in life by one, Jesus Christ.)

2 Corinthians 8:2 How that in a great trial of affliction the abundance of their joy and their deep poverty abounded unto the riches of their liberality.

2 Corinthians 8:14 But by an equality, that now at this time your abundance may be a supply for their want, that their abundance also may be a supply for your want: that there may be equality:

2 Corinthians 8:20 Avoiding this, that no man should blame us in this abundance which is administered by us:

2 Corinthians 12:7 And lest I should be exalted above measure through the abundance of the revelations, there was given to me a thorn in the flesh, the messenger of Satan to buffet me, lest I should be exalted above measure.

Revelations 18:3 For all nations have drunk of the wine of the wrath of her fornication, and the kings of the earth have committed fornication with her, and the merchants of the earth are waxed rich through the abundance of her delicacies.

RICHES

OLD TESTAMENT

Genesis 31:16 For all the riches which God hath taken from our father, that is ours, and our children's: now then, whatsoever God hath said unto thee, do.

Genesis 36:7 For their riches were more than that they might dwell together; and the land wherein they were strangers could not bear them because of their cattle.

Joshua 22:8 And he spake unto them, saying, Return with much riches unto your tents, and with very much cattle, with silver, and with gold, and with brass, and with iron, and with very much raiment: divide the spoil of your enemies with your brethren.

1 Samuel 17:25 And the men of Israel said, Have ye seen this man that is come up? surely to defy Israel is he come up: and it shall be, that the man who killeth him, the king will enrich him with great riches, and will give him his daughter, and make his father's house free in Israel.

1 Kings 3:11 And God said unto him, Because thou hast asked this thing, and hast not asked for thyself long life; neither hast asked riches for thyself, nor hast asked the life of thine enemies; but hast asked for thyself understanding to discern judgment;

1 Kings 3:13 And I have also given thee that which thou hast not asked, both riches, and honour: so that there shall not be any among the kings like unto thee all thy days.

1 Kings 10:23 So king Solomon exceeded all the kings of the earth for riches and for wisdom.

1 Chronicles 29:12 Both riches and honour come of thee, and thou reignest over all; and in thine hand is power and might; and in thine hand it is to make great, and to give strength unto all.

1 Chronicles 29:28 And he died in a good old age, full of days, riches, and honour: and Solomon his son reigned in his stead.

2 Chronicles 1:11 And God said to Solomon, Because this was in thine heart, and thou hast not asked riches, wealth, or honour, nor the life of thine enemies, neither yet hast asked long life; but hast asked wisdom and knowledge for thyself, that thou mayest judge my people, over whom I have made thee king:

2 Chronicles 1:12 Wisdom and knowledge is granted unto thee; and I will give thee riches, and wealth, and honour, such as none of the kings have had that have been before thee, neither shall there any after thee have the like.

2 Chronicles 9:22 And king Solomon passed all the kings of the earth in riches and wisdom.

2 Chronicles 17:5 Therefore the LORD stablished the kingdom in his hand; and all Judah brought to Jehoshaphat presents; and he had riches and honour in abundance.

2 Chronicles 18:1 Now Jehoshaphat had riches and honour in abundance, and joined affinity with Ahab.

2 Chronicles 20:25 And when Jehoshaphat and his people came to take away the spoil of them, they found among them in abundance both riches with the dead bodies, and precious jewels, which they stripped off for themselves, more than they could carry away: and they were three days in gathering of the spoil, it was so much.

2 Chronicles 32:27 And Hezekiah had exceeding much riches and honour: and he made himself treasuries for silver, and for gold, and for precious stones, and for spices, and for shields, and for all manner of pleasant jewels;

Esther 1:4 When he shewed the riches of his glorious kingdom and the honour of his excellent majesty many days, even an hundred and fourscore days.

Esther 5:11 And Haman told them of the glory of his riches, and the multitude of his children, and all the things wherein the king had promoted him, and how he had advanced him above the princes and servants of the king.

Job 20:15 He hath swallowed down riches, and he shall vomit them up again: God shall cast them out of his belly.

Job 36:19 Will he esteem thy riches? no, not gold, nor all the forces of strength.

Psalms 37:16 A little that a righteous man hath is better than the riches of many wicked.

Psalms 39:6 Surely every man walketh in a vain shew: surely they are disquieted in vain: he heapeth up riches, and knoweth not who shall gather them.

Psalms 49:6 They that trust in their wealth, and boast themselves in the multitude of their riches;

Psalms 52:7 Lo, this is the man that made not God his strength; but trusted in the abundance of his riches, and strengthened himself in his wickedness.

Psalms 62:10 Trust not in oppression, and become not vain in robbery: if riches increase, set not your heart upon them.

Psalms 73:12 Behold, these are the ungodly, who prosper in the world; they increase in riches.

Psalms 104:24 O LORD, how manifold are thy works! in wisdom hast thou made them all: the earth is full of thy riches.

Psalms 112:3 Wealth and riches shall be in his house: and his righteousness endureth for ever.

Psalms 119:14 I have rejoiced in the way of thy testimonies, as much as in all riches.

Proverbs 3:16 Length of days is in her right hand; and in her left hand riches and honour.

Proverbs 8:18 Riches and honour are with me; yea, durable riches and righteousness.

Proverbs 11:4 Riches profit not in the day of wrath: but righteousness delivereth from death.

Proverbs 11:16 A gracious woman retaineth honour: and strong men retain riches.

Proverbs 11:28 He that trusteth in his riches shall fall: but the righteous shall flourish as a branch.

Proverbs 13:7 There is that maketh himself rich, yet hath nothing: there is that maketh himself poor, yet hath great riches.

Proverbs 13:8 The ransom of a man's life are his riches: but the poor heareth not rebuke.

Proverbs 14:24 The crown of the wise is their riches: but the foolishness of fools is folly.

Proverbs 19:14 House and riches are the inheritance of fathers: and a prudent wife is from the LORD.

Proverbs 22:1 A good name is rather to be chosen than great riches, and loving favour rather than silver and gold.

Proverbs 22:4 By humility and the fear of the LORD are riches, and honour, and life.

Proverbs 22:16 He that oppresseth the poor to increase his riches, and he that giveth to the rich, shall surely come to want.

Proverbs 23:5 Wilt thou set thine eyes upon that which is not? for riches certainly make themselves wings; they fly away as an eagle toward heaven.

Proverbs 24:4 And by knowledge shall the chambers be filled with all precious and pleasant riches.

Proverbs 27:24 For riches are not for ever: and doth the crown endure to every generation?

Proverbs 30:8 Remove far from me vanity and lies: give me neither poverty nor riches; feed me with food convenient for me:

Ecclesiastes 4:8 There is one alone, and there is not a second; yea, he hath neither child nor brother: yet is there no end of all his labour; neither is his eye satisfied with riches; neither saith he, For whom do I labour, and bereave my soul of good? This is also vanity, yea, it is a sore travail.

Ecclesiastes 5:13 There is a sore evil which I have seen under the sun, namely, riches kept for the owners thereof to their hurt.

Ecclesiastes 5:14 But those riches perish by evil travail: and he begetteth a son, and there is nothing in his hand.

Ecclesiastes 5:19 Every man also to whom God hath given riches and wealth, and hath given him power to eat thereof, and to take his portion, and to rejoice in his labour; this is the gift of God.

Ecclesiastes 6:2 A man to whom God hath given riches, wealth, and honour, so that he wanteth nothing for his soul of all that he desireth, yet God giveth him not power to eat thereof, but a stranger eateth it: this is vanity, and it is an evil disease.

Ecclesiastes 9:11 I returned, and saw under the sun, that the race is not to the swift, nor the battle to the strong, neither yet bread to the wise, nor yet riches to men of understanding, nor yet favour to men of skill; but time and chance happeneth to them all.

Isaiah 8:4 For before the child shall have knowledge to cry, My father, and my mother, the riches of Damascus and the spoil of Samaria shall be taken away before the king of Assyria.

Isaiah 10:14 And my hand hath found as a nest the riches of the people: and as one gathereth eggs that are left, have I gathered all the earth; and there was none that moved the wing, or opened the mouth, or peeped.

Isaiah 30:6 The burden of the beasts of the south: into the land of trouble and anguish, from whence come the young and old lion, the viper and fiery flying serpent, they will carry their riches upon the shoulders of young asses, and their treasures upon the bunches of camels, to a people that shall not profit them.

Isaiah 45:3 And I will give thee the treasures of darkness, and hidden riches of secret places, that thou mayest know that I, the LORD, which call thee by thy name, am the God of Israel.

Isaiah 61:6 But ye shall be named the Priests of the LORD: men shall call you the Ministers of our God: ye shall eat the riches of the Gentiles, and in their glory shall ye boast yourselves.

Jeremiah 9:23 Thus saith the LORD, Let not the wise man glory in his wisdom, neither let the mighty man glory in his might, let not the rich man glory in his riches:

Jeremiah 17:11 As the partridge sitteth on eggs, and hatcheth them not; so he that getteth riches, and not by right, shall leave them in the midst of his days, and at his end shall be a fool.

Jeremiah 48:36 Therefore mine heart shall sound for Moab like pipes, and mine heart shall sound like pipes for the men of Kirheres: because the riches that he hath gotten are perished.

Ezekiel 26:12 And they shall make a spoil of thy riches, and make a prey of thy merchandise: and they shall break down thy walls, and destroy thy pleasant houses: and they shall lay thy stones and thy timber and thy dust in the midst of the water.

Ezekiel 27:12 Tarshish was thy merchant by reason of the multitude of all kind of riches; with silver, iron, tin, and lead, they traded in thy fairs.

Ezekiel 27:18 Damascus was thy merchant in the multitude of the wares of thy making, for the multitude of all riches; in the wine of Helbon, and white wool.

Ezekiel 27:27 Thy riches, and thy fairs, thy merchandise, thy mariners, and thy pilots, thy calkers, and the occupiers of thy merchandise, and all thy men of war, that are in thee, and in all thy company which is in the midst of thee, shall fall into the midst of the seas in the day of thy ruin.

Ezekiel 27:33 When thy wares went forth out of the seas, thou filledst many people; thou didst enrich the kings of the earth with the multitude of thy riches and of thy merchandise.

Ezekiel 28:4 With thy wisdom and with thine understanding thou hast gotten thee riches, and hast gotten gold and silver into thy treasures:

Ezekiel 28:5 By thy great wisdom and by thy traffick hast thou increased thy riches, and thine heart is lifted up because of thy riches:

Daniel 11:2 And now will I shew thee the truth. Behold, there shall stand up yet three kings in Persia; and the fourth shall be far richer than they all: and by his strength through his riches he shall stir up all against the realm of Grecia.

Daniel 11:13 For the king of the north shall return, and shall set forth a multitude greater than the former, and shall certainly come after certain years with a great army and with much riches.

Daniel 11:24 He shall enter peaceably even upon the fattest places of the province; and he shall do that which his fathers have not done, nor his fathers' fathers; he shall scatter among them the prey, and spoil, and riches: yea, and he shall forecast his devices against the strong holds, even for a time.

Daniel 11:28 Then shall he return into his land with great riches; and his heart shall be against the holy covenant; and he shall do exploits, and return to his own land.

NEW TESTAMENT

Matthew 13:22 He also that received seed among the thorns is he that heareth the word; and the care of this world, and the deceitfulness of riches, choke the word, and he becometh unfruitful.

Mark 4:19 And the cares of this world, and the deceitfulness of riches, and the lusts of other things entering in, choke the word, and it becometh unfruitful.

Mark 10:23 And Jesus looked round about, and saith unto his disciples, How hardly shall they that have riches enter into the kingdom of God!

Mark 10:24 And the disciples were astonished at his words. But Jesus answereth again, and saith unto them, Children, how hard is it for them that trust in riches to enter into the kingdom of God!

Luke 8:14 And that which fell among thorns are they, which, when they have heard, go forth, and are choked with cares and riches and pleasures of this life, and bring no fruit to perfection.

Luke 16:11 If therefore ye have not been faithful in the unrighteous mammon, who will commit to your trust the true riches?

Luke 18:24 And when Jesus saw that he was very sorrowful, he said, How hardly shall they that have riches enter into the kingdom of God!

Romans 2:4 Or despisest thou the riches of his goodness and forbearance and longsuffering; not knowing that the goodness of God leadeth thee to repentance?

Romans 9:23 And that he might make known the riches of his glory on the vessels of mercy, which he had afore prepared unto glory,

Romans 11:12 Now if the fall of them be the riches of the world, and the diminishing of them the riches of the Gentiles; how much more their fulness?

Romans 11:33 O the depth of the riches both of the wisdom and knowledge of God! how unsearchable are his judgments, and his ways past finding out!

2 Corinthians 8:2 How that in a great trial of affliction the abundance of their joy and their deep poverty abounded unto the riches of their liberality.

Ephesians 1:7 In whom we have redemption through his blood, the forgiveness of sins, according to the riches of his grace;

Ephesians 1:18 The eyes of your understanding being enlightened; that ye may know what is the hope of his calling, and what the riches of the glory of his inheritance in the saints,

Ephesians 2:7 That in the ages to come he might shew the exceeding riches of his grace in his kindness toward us through Christ Jesus.

Ephesians 3:8 Unto me, who am less than the least of all saints, is this grace given, that I should preach among the Gentiles the unsearchable riches of Christ;

Ephesians 3:16 That he would grant you, according to the riches of his glory, to be strengthened with might by his Spirit in the inner man;

Philippians 4:19 But my God shall supply all your need according to his riches in glory by Christ Jesus.

Colossians 1:27 To whom God would make known what is the riches of the glory of this mystery among the Gentiles; which is Christ in you, the hope of glory:

Colossians 2:2 That their hearts might be comforted, being knit together in love, and unto all riches of the full assurance of understanding, to the acknowledgement of the mystery of God, and of the Father, and of Christ;

1Timothy 6:17 Charge them that are rich in this world, that they be not highminded, nor trust in uncertain riches, but in the living God, who giveth us richly all things to enjoy;

Hebrews 11:26 Esteeming the reproach of Christ greater riches than the treasures in Egypt: for he had respect unto the recompence of the reward.

James 5:2 Your riches are corrupted, and your garments are motheaten.

Revelations 5:12 Saying with a loud voice, Worthy is the Lamb that was slain to receive power, and riches, and wisdom, and strength, and honour, and glory, and blessing.

Revelations 18:17 For in one hour so great riches is come to nought. And every shipmaster, and all the company in ships, and sailors, and as many as trade by sea, stood afar off,

www.ingramcontent.com/pod-product-compliance
Lightning Source LLC
Chambersburg PA
CBHW070751050426
42449CB00010B/2428